HOMEMADE BEER·CIDER AND STOUT

TIGER BOOKS INTERNATIONAL
LONDON

Contents

3292
This edition published in 1993 by Tiger Books International PLC, London
© 1993 CLB Publishing, Godalming, Surrey
Printed and bound in Singapore by Tien Wah Press
ISBN 1-85501-349-5

History of Beer

Beer is one of the oldest known alcoholic drinks, and one of the most popular in modern times. It has changed immeasurably since the pre-Christian era, but still depends on the same basic principles for its manufacture.

There is evidence of beer-making in Babylon as long ago as 6,000 BC, though it is not now certain that malted grains were the only ingredients; dates, honey etc. may have been included in the brews. Barley and emmer, a primitive form of wheat, were malted and boiled to produce a syrupy extract that could be stored. When needed, this syrup was diluted with water and fermented with yeast to form a type of unhopped beer, or ale, which was probably flavoured with herbs to help preserve it.

The god Osiris was said to have given beer to the ancient Egyptians about two thousand years before Christ, and the beer then was made by bakers, who crushed and soft baked the crudely malted grains and yeast, producing cakes that could be stored until required. These were then broken up in water and left to ferment, producing a cloudy and probably sweet weak ale. This technique was still followed in modern times among the peasants of Egypt, who produced 'Bouzah' at home. This is thought to have given rise to the common English term for a public house, the 'Boozer'.

Ale has been made since at least Anglo-Saxon times in Great Britain, from malted barley and water, fermented originally with baker's yeast, flavoured and preserved with a variety of herbs and wild flowers, such as bog myrtle and ivy. In Scandinavia a type of lichen growing wild on oak trees has been used to give ales a bitter taste. Flavourings for ale were so much in demand that at one time only the Church could sell 'gruit', a blend of herbs that was much favoured in Europe.

Hops were used in the Middle East and Asia Minor as a flavouring in pre-Christian days, and the use of this herb spread across Europe through Greek and Roman trading routes. Hops appeared in Germany at least as long ago as the 8th century, but it was not until the 16th century that hops are supposed to have come into England. It was over a hundred years before their use was fully accepted, but eventually the hop reigned supreme and beer, not ale, became the standard drink in Britain. Domestic water supplies in past centuries was frequently drawn from suspect sources, shallow and contaminated wells providing much in the way of disease-promoting water. Because of this, beers and ales formed a large part of the daily beverages for all ages and classes, from children upwards, and consequently were made in a variety of strengths. As well as being a safe thirst-quencher, beer provided vitamins, protein and minerals, and became an essential supplement to the poor diet of the greater part of the population, especially in the winter and early spring.

In the Middle Ages ale and beer was made at home, mostly by women maltsters and brewsters – and it was not until the 17th and 18th centuries that commercial maltings and breweries sprang up to supply beer to those who found it easier to buy standardised, but efficiently produced, beers for sale or consumption than to spend time making small quantities of different beers themselves, and risking loss through spoilage into the bargain. The great brewery dynasties were started then, such as Truman's, Whitbread's, and Guinness. At first this meant a

greater variety of beers becoming available to the public. Since then there has been a continuous decline in the range, due to amalgamations and thus reductions in the number of small, independent breweries. Half a dozen major combines now produce about three quarters of Britain's beer. The loss of choice and drop in quality became so pronounced in post-war years that in 1971 the Campaign for Real Ale (CAMRA) was formed. This consumers' pressure group has been signally successful in convincing the big brewers that there is market for good quality beers, as opposed to a sort of standard Euro-keg chilled fizz, and many good beers are now on sale again. There are, of course, still a number of independent smaller concerns that have always sold good beer, and names like Adnams, Gibbs Mew, and Greenall Whitley will always bring a sparkle both to a beer-drinker's glass and his eye!

So why bother with home brewing? Brewing beer can be a fascinating hobby, and there is undoubtedly a great financial saving to be made in producing your own beer at home. At a time when publicans commonly charge over £1 for a pint of bitter, a mug of excellent, home-brewed beer from a top-quality kit costs about 10p! An experienced home brewer making his or her beer from the raw materials will make beer for even less. And though your local hostelries may between them offer perhaps four or five different brews, at home you can make any type of beer you fancy. Thousands of recipes have been published, for beers made all over the world. So if you wish to try imitating a Pittsburgh or a Pilsener, a Grolsch or a Greene King, the opportunity is there, and you are not restricted to buying just a can or bottle.

It should also be remembered that home beermakers use the same ingredients as the professional commercial brewers; they are not restricted by accountants with watchful eye on fractions of a penny, nor responsible to managers with their marketing worries and deadlines to meet. Making beer at home is a labour of love, and the excellence of the end product rests largely with the home brewer and the 'tender loving care' that can be lavished on the hobby. Home-made beers can be – indeed, should be – every bit as good as most brewery beers, and the better beers will stand comparison with anything made commercially.

Disadvantages ? There is only one general point that may be described as a drawback, and that is usually voiced by the housewife rather than the husband! It does make the house smell a little like a brewery, but that, of course, is precisely what it is. And it is only for an hour or so, during the initial process, with perhaps a lesser background hint of beer to the room for a day or so during fermentation. But the finished product justifies any slight distraction that the brewing process might cause. A lesser factor is that in different area the water and its dissolved minerals vary, so occasionally it is advisable to adjust the water when making particular types of beer.

Well, after all that, just what is beer ? A detailed description of malting and brewing will follow later, but the basic process is fairly simple: barley grain is malted, which just means that it is kept warm and moist, so that germination commences. As soon as this happens the barley is dried in an oven to stop further growth. It is then coarsely ground, and simmered in water at a set temperature until enzymes in the grain have converted all the starch to sugar. Drained off, the liquid is boiled up with hops, cooled, and yeast is added. This ferments the sweet liquid (wort), the yeast producing lots more yeast, carbon dioxide gas, and alcohol. Clarified and matured – that's beer!

Of course, like all apparently simple manufacturing processes, there's more to it than that, but whatever the beer is, and regardless of who makes it, or where, the basic process stays unchanged. If you start beermaking with a kit, (and that is all that most home brewers use,) then it is almost as easy as making instant coffee – and with an end product nearer to the original!

And just like the commercial brews, home made beers can be draught, under gas pressure from a keg, or bottled in glass or P.E.T. plastic bottles. Some home brewers have beer pumps, filtration equipment, beer coolers, pressure systems, and build bars in their homes, but these are not essentials for making or serving an enjoyable drink. Seven or eight 3-litre plastic beer or lemonade containers will hold a five gallon brew, and you can serve bright, sparkling beers, lagers and stouts to your friends and family with no difficulty at all. Home canning of beer is not practicable at present, and not generally desirable anyway.

There are several different types of beer on the market, all of which can be made by the amateur at home. In brief, beer in the UK usually means a beer made with our native top-fermenting yeast, which produces masses of stiff foam on top of the vat, containing a high proportion of surplus yeast. This applies to bitter, mild, brown, pale ale and porter. Stouts are made in the same way, with the same style of yeast, but with some unmalted roasted barley to give a dark colour and burnt flavour.

Lagers are fermented with a different strain of yeast, which does not form the same surface effect, but which sinks to the bottom of the vat. Lagers are (or should be) stored for some weeks longer than top-fermented beers before being sold, 'lager' being from the German word for storage. These are the drinks sold as beers throughout most of the world. They are often made with maize (corn) and other grains, especially outside Europe.

The ingredients for home beermaking are normally easily obtained. Kits containing either dried malt extract or malt syrup and flavoured with hop extract are on sale in every homebrew shop, some multiple stores, chemists and supermarkets. The raw materials, such as hops, grains, loose-pack or canned malt extracts, yeasts etc., are sold mostly in homebrew and some health food shops. As these ingredients can vary in quality, and some deteriorate quickly with age or poor storage, it pays to buy from a specialist shop that can be expected to have a rapid turnover, and knows how to look after stock.

The materials for making beer at home, either as complete kits or as separate ingredients, are not expensive, and the capital outlay on equipment can be just a few pounds. A space at room temperature in which to stand a fermenting bin, and somewhere to store the bottles or a keg when the beer is finished, are all that is needed. The time taken is negligible, perhaps an hour to get the brew under way, an occasional five minutes' attention, and perhaps an hour to bottle or keg the finished beer. To ferment the beer usually takes about a week, and three weeks is ideal for maturing and conditioning the finished beer, though it can be drunk younger if you are desperate. So you can see that home brewing is not expensive, it is easy to do, does not take up a lot of your time, and is ready in a matter of weeks. Why not take that first step, and make a beer of your own?

Beer Equipment

Basic Needs

What equipment do you need to make your first few pints of beer? Very little. The process of making a gallon or two of excellent homebrew from a malt extract or a commercial kit is quite simple, so you will not need expensive or complicated equipment.

Let us assume you are starting with a typical commercial beermaking kit, consisting of a can containing malt extract syrup, flavoured with hop extract, and with a packet of beer yeast under an outer lid, to make two gallons of beer.

Obviously you need a tin opener (the usual butterfly-nut opener found in the kitchen is ideal), and a sterile bucket in which to ferment the diluted beer materials – known as the wort (rhyming with shirt, not short!). This should be new, food grade white plastic, fitted with a lid, and never used for any other purpose – not even winemaking. You may have to heat the malt, or dissolve some sugar in water, so a large saucepan and something to stir with will be needed. The beer has to be bottled, so you will want a few screw-top P.E.T. plastic bottles, the containers that beer, cider, and lemonade come in. If you want to bottle in glass, then the bottles must be the strong, returnable glass bottles used for beer or other fizzy drinks; non-returnable bottles are designed to be short lived, and are dangerous to reuse. Most glass beer bottles today are sealed with crown caps, so you will require a supply of crowns and a capping tool. A simple tool to be used with a mallet or hammer need cost only two to three pounds. Plastic re-seal caps can also be bought cheaply for this type of bottle. Finally, you will want a length of clear plastic tubing to syphon the beer from the fermenting bucket to the bottles, and a bottle brush for cleaning. So, to summarise, the essentials will probably be:-

tin opener
saucepan
large spoon
bucket with lid
syphon
bottles and closures
cleaning brush.

The first three items are probably in your kitchen already, and bottles can be accumulated by saving empties. If you want to buy new glass bottles, your local homebrew shop will stock them. That just leaves the bucket, bottle brush, and the syphon, and these should also come from a homebrew supplier to ensure the correct quality. There are two very useful pieces of equipment that, although not essential, do make home brewing a little easier.

The first is a **thermometer**, which will tell you accurately when the wort is cool enough for the yeast to be added, and can also be used to check that the brew is being kept at a suitable temperature. Do buy a brewing and wine making thermometer from your homebrew supplier; the clinical thermometer used for checking the children's temperatures, the long one you use for jam-making, and that dusty thing hanging in the greenhouse are all quite unsuited to the making of beer.

The second item is actually two; a **test jar** and an **hydrometer**. The test jar is simply used to hold a sample of wort or beer to be tested by the hydrometer. The hydrometer is floated in the test jar, and by the height it projects above the liquid you can tell the sugar strength of the wort, or how the fermentation is progressing. The hydrometer is an easy tool to use, and is dealt with at greater length later.

For a Bigger Brew

Most kits on sale are for making five gallons of beer, a good round figure of forty pints. This may seem a lot, but your stock will not last long if you have thirsty friends and relations calling during a hot summer. In any case, a good beer will keep for months as long as it is kept cool and sealed in bottle, or well-cared for in a keg.

The obvious differences are that you will need a larger pan, but one that holds a gallon will be sufficient, and a longer-handled spoon; homebrew shops sell plastic spoons specially made for the job. The fermenting bin needs to be large enough to hold five or six gallons, again with a lid. And for the beer, when it is made, you will require more bottles, or alternatively a plastic barrel or keg. (Strictly, a barrel holds 36 gallons, which is a bit beyond most people's scope).

Plastic kegs are made specially for the hobby, usually to hold five gallons. Make sure it is a suitable grade of plastic, has a wide mouth that you can get your hand in for ease of cleaning – and cleaning is very important – and has a screw cap at the top and a tap fitted near the bottom. In addition, you need a fitting to take a carbon dioxide (CO_2) bottle to stop the beer going off in the keg. These are readily available, and either take a Sparklet or similar small gas bulb, or a larger bottle made specifically for the task. The gas prevents non-sterile air from contaminating the beer, and helps it flow more readily from the tap. So:

5-gallon fermenter
larger pan
long-handled spoon
extra bottles, or
keg and fittings
gas (CO_2)
For a Bigger Brew Using Grain Malt

So far we have looked at equipment using malt extracts, but the very best home-made beers follow the professional brewers and use crushed grain malt barley rather than malt syrups or dried malt powders. Most good homebrew shops sell crushed malt barley ready for use, but if you cannot buy ready-crushed malt you will want a coarse-bladed mincer or a coffee-mill that gives a coarse-particled product. Additionally, as the crushed grains and hops will need straining from the wort at varying stages, there is need for a straining cloth, either muslin or nylon, or a similar synthetic such as terylene curtaining. Apart from these two items, the equipment remains the same.

Supplementary

All the above equipment needs to be more than just clean by kitchen standards. Total sterility is the aim for surgical operating theatres, and beyond amateur capability, but there is no excuse for beer going off either in the making or afterwards. Beer wort is an ideal medium for all sorts of bacteria, moulds and wild yeasts to breed in, and finished beer is always receptive to attacks by spoilage organisms of many sorts. There is little point in making a complex, and possibly expensive, beer wort just to have it turned into malt vinegar or worse through

carelessness. Spoilage organisms are waiting in the air, twenty-four hours a day, to colonise your precious brew and ruin it.

This may sound an unhappy state of affairs, but the invaders are easily repelled. All equipment must be sterilised with a cleansing medium, but soap (or detergent) and water are not enough. Boiling water is a good disinfectant, but cannot be certain to reach every crevice for long enough to kill off the bacteria etc. There are several excellent chlorine-based sterilants on the homebrew market that will make a perfect job of getting rid of unwanted micro-organisms, as well as acting as a general cleaner, if used according to the maker's instructions. Such chemicals need to be rinsed away afterwards with plenty of fresh water to avoid giving the beer an off-flavour. Campden tablets, or sodium (or potassium) metabisulphite can be used instead, but the supply must be fresh: Campden tablets and sulphite solutions deteriorate quite quickly once opened and exposed to light or air.

Additional Equipment

As you progress in your brewing as a hobby, you will find there are numerous pieces of equipment that are not essential, but are used by enthusiasts to give that finishing touch to their homebrewed beers, stouts, and lagers. Fermenting temperatures can be guaranteed in the coldest weather by using an electrically-powered heating pad or belt beneath or around your fermenting bucket or bin. Power filtration can give clearer beers from the keg, and miniature hand pumps can be fitted to a keg to draw off draught beer. There are plastic spanners to tighten or loosen keg screw caps, handles to ease moving kegs, and even jackets for kegs that will take freezer packs to chill a finished beer. The range of equipment to help the home brewer emulate the professional is growing continually.

The Brewing Process

After reading this chapter, the novice brewer or brewster may think the whole business is too complicated. Don't be put off! Most homebrewed beers are made using the simplest of recipes, or from branded kits, and are easy, trouble-free operations, no more complex than the great majority of kitchen routines. But you might later wonder what some of these strange substances are that your homebrew shop sells, or that you find mentioned in other recipes, so read what is printed, and carry on regardless. It will help you to understand the brewing process, and your memory will remind you that there is something about, say, carragheen or invert sugar when the need arises, and it is there for reference.

As already mentioned, the malting of barley grain consists mainly of inducing the grain to produce enzymes that modify the starch, in which the plant has stored energy, so that later it can be converted into sugars that the beer yeast can feed on. The malting is then halted by heating the malt, the malted grain reduced to grist by lightly crushing it, and the malt is then ready for the brewer to use.

Barley malt comes in a variety of colours, ranging from a pale, creamy shade hardly any darker than the raw grain, to a soft black. The colour depends on how fiercely the malt is kilned after the malting process. Pale malt is the normal malt used for pale ales and bitters, and frequently for lager as well. There is, however, a special lager malt. Dark malt is a few shades browner, and is suitable for brown ales and milds.

Chocolate malt has been ovened to a greater degree still, and was used to give a beer more colour and flavour. It is no longer common. Patent black malt – the patent probably ran out in the last century – is malt that has been carbonified in the kiln. It has a harsh, burnt flavour, and used to be a favourite malt to beef up stouts and porters. It, too, is now little used.

Crystal malt is malt that has been processed until the sugar inside the husk has melted and crystallised like toffee. It is popular for giving beers colour and a malty flavour, needing only to be lightly crushed and boiled in water to extract the soluble sugar crystals.

Roasted barley has largely replaced patent black in stout making. It is unmalted grain, simply roasted until it is of a suitable shade of brown to satisfy the brewer. Roasted barley can be bought from specialist homebrew shops, or prepared in the kitchen oven in a shallow layer in a roasting tin.

It must be remembered that the dark malts have been caramelised to a certain extent, and do not contain any living enzymes that can be used to help mash other unmalted grains. Fortunately, beers are not usually made from these malts alone; they are normally included as a minor proportion of the total malt used for a mash, to enhance colour and flavour.

The process of extracting the maltose and other sugars from the crushed malt (grist) is one of simmering a porridge of ground malt and water at carefully controlled temperatures, around 150°F (64°C). This is because differing

temperatures cause different enzyme reactions, which affects the proportions of the different malt sugars, mainly maltose, sucrose and dextrin, that are produced. These proportions eventually affect the character of the beer itself. For example, a high dextrin beer will be fairly full bodied as the yeast cannot feed on this sugar as easily. Happily the home brewer is not particularly affected by these abstruse complications, as the great majority of homebrewers use kits or malt extracts where the cooking (mashing) of the malt has already been carried out by specialist maltsters. For those using malted grain, only the keen, competitive brewer is likely to notice the slight difference made by the variation of a degree or two of temperature in the mashing process.

Approximately 150°F will give the homebrewer the optimum conditions for the conversion of starch to sugars, and the enzymes in the mash can be used to convert additional starchy substances. As an example, corn (maize) and rice in various forms are often used to lighten a beer in texture and colour, but in this country are supplied unmalted. Cooked in with the mash of malt and water, this extra starchy material is converted to fermentable sugars by the surplus enzymes from the malt. Without the enzymes, and at higher temperatures, the added grain would simply gelatinize and make a useless sticky pudding.

After the mashing period – up to an hour or even more – the mash is strained to extract the sugar-laden liquid, the 'wort'. The remaining solids are then 'sparged' (another lovely old-fashioned word). Brewing is full of such antique words, simply because it is such an ancient craft. Sparging is simply the practice of spraying the residues with hot water to wash the last of the sugars out of the grain husks, and ensure the whole of the wort is extracted.

It is, however, far easier for the homebrewer to buy the malt sugars already extracted from the grain malt by specialist firms, or maltsters. Malt extract can be bought as a sticky syrup (without cod liver oil) in varying grades. Always make sure you buy a diastatic brewing grade, which still contains some enzymes, or the malt extract powder. The latter has the advantage of coming in several shades of colour, which is most useful in making different beers, such as a pale ale or a dark mild. It has lost its water through a vacuum process, and is very hygroscopic. In other words, it must be kept sealed from the air until it is used, or it will pick up moisture and turn into a sort of toffee-like block that is quite slow to dissolve in hot water. As it is dried, only four fifths the amount by weight is needed, compared to malt syrup. The wort, whether from malt grain or from dried or syrup malt extract, is then boiled up with the hops.

Hops are the flowers of a climbing plant, the hop bine, that is trained to grow up wires. Most English hops come from Kent, Worcestershire or Herefordshire, should be soft to the touch, and a delicate pale green-gold in colour. Rub them between your palms and smell the clean, strong aroma of the lupulin from the flowers; this is the main bittering agent of the hops. Dry, brittle and yellowed hops are old and spoiled, and should be avoided as far as brewing is concerned. Hops are supposed to help bring refreshing sleep, so if you accidentally keep your hops too long and they spoil, pop them in a cloth bag to make a hop pillow; it may bring relaxation on a restless night, or the rustling noise may keep you awake!. Otherwise, throw them away.

The inclusion of hops in beer is mainly to prevent deterioration; the resins in the hops discourage bacterial growth and lessen the chances of the beer being spoiled. The hops also help give the beer that fine aroma and flavour, as well as helping the beer to clear rapidly. Lastly, hops act as a diuretic, so you can always claim you only drink beer for the wellbeing of your kidneys. The hops are strained out after the boiling, but extra hops are often added to the beer as it is put in barrels or kept to mature, and this is known as 'dry-hopping'. It just adds a little extra tanginess to the beer.

Recipes sometimes suggest using Saaz or Hallertauer hops; these are varieties grown on the Continent, where the male plant has largely been eradicated. The hops are stronger in use, partly because there are no seeds adding useless weight, and they add a slightly different taste and nose to the beer. They are mostly used in making lagers, which are of course the commonest beers made in Europe. There are many British hop varieties, but the commonest by far are the Goldings, used for pale ales and bitters, and Fuggles, used in brown ales and mild beer. Most of the others are hybrids and sub-strains (e.g; East Kent Goldings, commonly known as E.K.Gs), bred to try to improve some particular characteristic.

Water – liquor to the trade – is the main ingredient of any beer, and can be a major source of difficulty due to the minerals dissolved in it; these vary from place to place. Burton pale ales and bitters are famous, and the water there is high in sulphates; London is known for its mild and brown ale, and was once famed for its porter, a soft stout-type beer, all of which are best made with soft water. In most cases, the homebrewer need not bother about adjusting the water he uses, but if you aim for perfection in your beer – and you should – a simple way of increasing sulphates is to add two teaspoons of Epsom salts (magnesium sulphate) and one of salt (sodium chloride) to each five gallons of water, and if your water furs the kettle, half a teaspoon of citric acid. The chalky, hard-water minerals, mostly carbonates, are largely lost during the boiling and straining processes. Water from chalky sources has only 'temporary' hardness; the 'permanent' hardness of sulphates is generally an advantage. If you would like an an analysis of your water, the water authority will provide you with one, usually free of charge, on request.

Yeast is the last major factor in brewing. Yeasts are single-cell fungi (saccharomyces cerevisae) that feed on sugars, releasing carbon dioxide and alcohol as by products.

Commercially the carbon dioxide gas is recovered and used for putting the fizz in bottled beer. The homebrewer lets it escape into the air and provides it in other ways to serve his beer, as explained later. Beer yeast is a long-established variant of bread yeast, and has gradually been selected for providing alcohol in preference to carbon dioxide gas for raising dough. Brewers' yeast is pitched (added to the cooled wort) and signs of activity are normally visible within twenty four hours. After a day or so the yeast will have thrown up a thick foam, stiff with surplus yeast, which in commerce is skimmed off for making savoury spreads and yeast extracts. The homebrewer generally skims the head off and discards it, as this also gets rid of some of the excess bitterness from the hops and reduces the chances of a yeasty-tasting beer. British beer yeasts throw out the bulk of the surplus yeast this way, and the rest sinks when the fermentation ends. Lager yeasts (saccharomyces c. carlsbergensis) are a specialised strain selected for lager brewing. Lager yeast may throw up a thick head which quickly subsides, and most of the fermentation takes place with yeast cells that sink at the end. Lager continues to ferment very slowly for some time after the turbulent part of the fermentation has ended, hence its name, which means 'storage', from its long maturation period.

Other sugars are added in many beer formulations, particularly beer kits. This is an economy measure and an easy way to raise the alcohol level. However, ordinary cane or beet sugar (sucrose) ferments away almost completely, so beers with too much added sugar tend to be thin and unbalanced. 'Invert' sugar is sugar that has been treated to break it down into roughly equal parts of glucose and fructose, and there is no point in paying extra for sticky blocks of sugar and water, when the yeast itself is capable of converting the sugar. Glucose is a sugar that has been converted with acid from starch, and comes as hard, dry lumps (glucose chips) or as wheat or corn syrup. Glucose tends to give a beer with a drier finish as it too ferments out almost completely. Recipes occasionally specify honey, brown sugar, syrup, treacle or molasses, but these types of sugar are only used to help give special flavours in the finished beer. Do not use them as a normal substitute for domestic sugar, unless you want a beer with a different taste and aroma. There is one other form of sugar occasionally used in home brewing, and that is burnt sugar, sold as caramel. Caramel is used to darken the colour of a beer, and has no other value. Domestic sugar can be caramelised by heating it in an old spoon over a gas flame, but it is much simpler, and you get a more consistent product, by buying a bottle of gravy browning. This may contain a little salt as well as the caramel, but not sufficient to affect the quality of your beer. Use it sparingly, adding perhaps a teaspoonful to five gallons and stirring well, before deciding whether the colour needs deepening further.

Beer, being made from a starchy material, can easily throw a haze if the conversion to sugars is not completed fully. This can easily be checked by putting a few drops of the liquid taken from the mash and spotting it on a piece of white tile. Add a drop or two of common tincture of iodine, and if there is starch still present in the wort the sample will turn blue. (Try this iodine test on a few drops of water that potatoes have been boiled in; you should get a dramatic response, with a deep indigo blue stain). As long as the iodine test shows the wort still contains starch, the mashing should continue, until conversion to maltose, dextrins etc. is complete.

One way of reducing the risk of hazes is to add finings to the boil of wort and hops. Copper finings, which are named after the brewery's boiling copper, not the metal called copper, are also known as Irish moss (which they are not), or carragheen; the latter is a dried Irish seaweed which, when boiled with the wort, helps to coagulate the unwanted proteins as the wort cools. The coagulated material falls harmlessly to the bottom of the beer.

Finished beer is often slow to clear ready for kegging or bottling, and a different type of finings can help here. Usually these are gelatin or isinglass finings, to be made up as the manufacturers instruct, and should make the beer fall bright within twenty-four to forty-eight hours. Do not fine with the bentonite that is recommended for wine-making, as it forms too thick a layer of sediment and wastes beer. And wasting beer is unforgiveable.

After fining the beer should be clear, fully fermented, and ready for bottling, or kegging as draught beer.

Bottles must be containers that have been made for holding liquids under pressure, such as beer, fizzy lemonade, or sparkling cider. Glass bottles must be free from scratches or chips, and scrupulously clean. Non-returnable bottles are not suitable; they are designed as one-trip bottles only, and may well give way under the gas pressure of well-conditioned beer. The P.E.T. plastic bottles now used commercially for one, two, or three litre packs are excellent, easily sterilised and filled, and perfectly safe. Always remember that the caps as well as the bottles need to be sterile. They can be scalded with boiling water or soaked in a strong Campden tablet solution. If the screw-in type of stoppe is used, make sure you remove the rubber ring and clean both stopper and ring before reassembly. If you are using ordinary crown-top bottles, seal them with new metal crown caps, using a capping tool, or with clip-on plastic seals.

Rack (syphon) the beer off the sediment carefully. Putting a rubber bung or similar small object under the back edge of the bin as a chock will help get the greatest amount of bright beer before the syphon starts sucking up the yeast. The brew needs a little extra sugar to ferment to provide 'conditioning', the secondary fermentation that produces enough carbon dioxide gas in solution to give the beer a nice head and sparkle when it is opened. Use a dry funnel to put half a teaspoon of sugar in each pint bottle, or easier still, for five gallons add four ounces of sugar dissolved in a little hot water to the brew, and stir thoroughly to make sure the

sugar is well mixed in. The beer can then be transferred with the syphon tube to the bottles, and the caps fitted. Put the bottles away in a warm spot for three or four days to get the secondary fermentation going, then store them in a cooler place to mature for about another three weeks. The beer is drinkable after the first few days, but storage gives it time to settle down and lose its rawness. The 'bead' (the lines of bubbles that rise) will also be finer after maturation, and this is always a sign of a well-kept beer.

There should be no more than a trace of yeast at the bottom of the bottle, but if the bottle is tipped for pouring part of the beer and then stood up again, the contents will swirl and the yeast will make the remainder of the beer temporarily cloudy. This is harmless, but to British eyes unsightly, and it is preferable to pour at one go all the beer you intend to serve on that occasion, even if this means using a jug.

Storing your beer in a keg is an alternative that calls for less labour, but a little more capital expenditure. Firstly, make sure that the cask is clean and sterilised, and that the bottom tap is closed. It is only too easy to leave it open when you have just cleaned it, and then distressing to be busily syphoning your precious brew into the top of the keg only to find that it is just as rapidly running out of the tap and all over the floor! Also the gas injector needs fitting to the cap before the beer is put into the keg, so that the cap is ready to screw down as soon as filling has taken place. A five-gallon brew can be syphoned into a keg, the conditioning sugar stirred in as a syrup, and the cap then screwed down to make an airtight seal so conditioning can commence. Kegged beer, due to its greater depth and volume, takes longer to clear after conditioning than bottled beer does, but you do have the convenience of being able to draw off a pint, or top up a glass, with no danger of disturbing the lees as happens with bottles.

After a few pints have been drawn off the flow from the tap will slow down, and this is when you fit a gas cartridge. The carbon dioxide gas released into the barrel prevents air and its attendant bacteria and wild yeasts being drawn into the barrel as the beer is drawn out, and helps to ensure an even flow from the tap. It is not intended to pressure feed the beer from the barrel, although there are taps that dispense from the barrel cap under gas pressure. These, of course, use a little more carbon dioxide gas. One last word of advice: breweries were always designed so that the ingredients were taken by hoist to the top of the brewery, and the water was pumped up to a reservoir near the roof. From there almost the whole process was by gravity feed. This was simply because beer in bulk is heavy, and it is worthwhile bearing this in mind when planning your home brewing. When the mash is finished, or the can of hopped malt, sugar and hot water have been put in the fermenting bin, raise it to a working height you can eventually syphon from, before you add the buckets of cold water needed to make the wort up to five gallons. And when you are racking the finished beer into a clean container or a keg, just half fill it, so that that, too, can comfortably be lifted up to your worktop. The rest of the brew can be syphoned off the yeast into one or more other containers, and then lifted and poured into the keg or bin. This has the advantage that if the fermenting bin slips or is otherwise disturbed, your syphon won't pour yeasty sediment into the whole of the brew. You will then have a shorter time to wait for the sediment to resettle so that syphoning can recommence.

Nowadays hop-picking is a mechanized process, of which the final stage is completely stripping the hop plants from the poles.

Kit Beers

Beer kits are many and extremely varied, but all have the same basic purpose: to put in the hands of the purchaser all, or most, of the ingredients necessary to make beer at home with the greatest possible ease. The manufacturers of kits have now succeeded so well that it is now possible to buy a kit that only need filling up with water and leaving until the beer is ready to drink.

Kits for sale to hobbyists first appeared just after World War II. Early beer kits typically consisted of a parcel or box containing a bag of dried malt extract, a handful of crystal malt to give the beer a malty taste and improve the colour, a few dried hops, and an envelope in which would be found a supply of dried beer yeast. All these ingredients except the yeast were boiled up in a pan of water and strained into a two-gallon bucket. A couple of pounds of sugar were usually stirred into the brew, but if this took the alcohol content of the beer to more than two percent – and it invariably did – the brewer had to obtain a brewing licence from the Customs and Excise. (Fortunately, the Chancellor of the Exchequer, Reginald Maudling, scrapped this iniquitous law in his budget of April 1963, leaving the homebrewer free to make as much beer, of any strength he or she liked, as long as it was for private consumption and not for sale).

Cold water was added to fill up the bucket, leaving a little space for foaming, and when all had cooled the yeast was sprinkled over the surface. The strain of yeast used in those days threw a heavy deposit as a dark brown ring round the bucket at surface level, and a thick, foaming head, also blotched with brown patches. It was essential to remove this brown scum and tidemark, or the beer would taste unpleasant, with a strange flavour known as 'yeast-bite'.

After the wort had fermented from five to seven days in the bucket, finings had to be added, and the beer racked off the sediment to avoid further off-flavours from the yeast. The beer was then bottled, with a little sugar added to each bottle to enliven the beer, and two or three weeks later it was ready to drink.

Kits of this type could make excellent beer, and many thousands of gallons were produced and drunk with relish. Unfortunately, all kits were not of a satisfactory standard, relying far too much on sugar to provide the alcohol, and with insufficient malt to make a satisfactory beer.

Homebrewing needs about a pound of malt and other sugars per gallon, and Hugh Semple, one of the hobby's trade pioneers, records checking a rival firm's kit and finding that it contained just eight ounces of dried malt, a small sachet of synthetic hop flavour, and instructions to add four pounds of sugar! Needless to say, such merchants did not stay in business very long. Dried ingredient kits have now been phased out by all the major manufacturers, who have slowly but consistently improved the contents of the kits they sell, and the average modern beer kit represents very good value for money. Most currently on sale will produce beer at from 10p to 15p a pint, with the average pint costing about 12p.

Pub beers vary in price throughout the country, with a national average of over £1 a pint. What more convincing reason could you have for making a few gallons of beer at home? Modern kits are virtually foolproof; many have been reviewed over the last few years, and a noticeable aspect of almost all of them has been the simplicity and clarity of the instructions.

The standard type of kit now on sale is in the form of a can containing about four pounds of concentrated wort, with the detailed instructions either on the reverse side of the label, or as a leaflet under a false lid to the can. Such lids frequently also contain a packet of brewing yeast, and occasionally a packet of finings. Where not provided, these have to be bought from a homebrew specialist supplier, and it is strongly recommended that you buy the best beer yeast available. It is false economy to pay £3 to £5 for a can of concentrate, and produce an inferior, or even spoiled, beer for the sake of saving a few pence on the yeast.

The majority of cans contain just 100 per cent malt extract, in the form of a dark, treacly syrup, flavoured with hops added before the evaporation of the water from the wort, or with hop extract. To these kits it is normal to add a kilo of granulated sugar to make a forty-pint brew. Some of the cheaper kits include a proportion of glucose syrup; this is normal commercial practice, even by the big brewers, but tends to produce a thinner, drier beer, especially if much domestic sugar has to be added as well.

The high quality of the beers produced by kits today is confirmed by the fact that several breweries now produce their own beer kits, or lend their names to kits produced to duplicate the beers from their breweries. This would be unthinkable if the kits could not make up into beer at least as good as that sold in public houses;

it would rapidly bring the brewery's name into disrepute. Coopers, the big Australian brewers, even export their excellent beer kits to the United Kingdom. And there are English public houses that make beer on the premises from just the same ingredients as those the amateur uses.

A typical set of instructions for making up a beer kit might be as follows. Explanatory comments are printed in italic.

1. Bring 4 pints of water to the boil in a large saucepan. *A jam-making pan is ideal if your pans are not big enough.*

2. Add the contents of the can, and a kilo of sugar. Stir well to dissolve and simmer for five minutes. *If you remove the can label, and then stand the can in a bowl of hot water for a few minutes, the malt extract will pour into the pan more easily. Rinse out the can with hot water, and tip this into your fermenting bin to avoid waste.*

3. Pour the contents of the pan into your fermenting bin, and make up to five gallons with cold tap water. Stir well; the temperature should now be below 75°F (24°C) and the yeast can be sprinkled on the surface. Cover with the bin lid or a thick cloth, and keep in a warm place. *A higher temperature might well kill the yeast. Do not stir the yeast into the beer, it needs oxygen from the air to start with, so it can multiply. A cover is essential to prevent contamination by wild yeasts, moulds and bacteria, which are prevalent in even the most well-kept household. Keep the beer at normal room temperature, about 65°-70°F (18°-21°C).*

4. Ferment the beer for five to seven days; the fermentation is almost finished when the beer starts clearing and few bubbles rise. A hydrometer reading should be between 1000-1005. Syphon the beer into bottles or a keg, after priming with half a teaspoon of sugar per pint. Leave an airspace of about three quarters of an inch between each bottle cap and the surface of the beer. *It is advisable to add finings as instructed by the manufacturer and syphon the beer off the sediment twenty-four hours later. The beer will then throw less sediment in the bottle and keep its flavour better. Dissolve four ounces of sugar in a little hot water, and stir this thoroughly into the beer before kegging or bottling, rather than trying to add dry sugar to each bottle. This priming sugar is to cause a secondary fermentation in the bottle or keg, so the beer will have a sparkle. There is, therefore, bound to be a little yeast sediment when the beer is finished.*

5. Store in a warm place for three days to condition, then remove to a cool store to mature for two weeks, or three weeks if in a barrel. *The beer has to be kept warm for a few days so that the trace of yeast it contains can multiply and ferment away the priming sugar. This will make the beer fizzy, from the carbon dioxide gas given off as a by-product from the yeast feeding on the sugar. Putting the beer in a cool place afterwards will help the yeast to drop to the bottom of the bottle or keg, and give the beer time to smooth off and mature. Three weeks maturation is preferable. A keg of beer will take a little longer than a bottle to clear and mature properly, due to the greater depth and volume involved.*

6. Serve the beer chilled – half an hour in the door of a refrigerator is sufficient – and pour it gently down the inside of the glass. *Make sure you keep the bottles upright to avoid disturbing the yeast, as this makes the beer look unsightly. If all the beer is not being poured into a single glass – for example, if you are pouring a half pint to try it – pour all the beer you can in one smooth movement into a jug, before the yeast rises, and dispense it from there. The second half pint will then be as clear as the first.*

Beers for Springtime

The days for 'winter warmers' have passed, though a cutting March wind can be a good excuse for a pint of good best bitter! Now is the time to think about making beers for a purpose – beers of specific types. There is no reason why you should not make a range of beers that are similar to those available commercially, so chapter by chapter the greater part of the beers styles that are made in the UK will be dealt with. No outlandish ingredients are needed: all beers are made by the samebasic process of a yeast fermenting the malt sugars released by the malting and mashing processes.

Pale ales are the aristocrats of British brewing. Made from the finest quality hops and malt, they are usually a pale gold in colour and, with a high starting gravity (high sugar content), they ferment out into crisp, dry beers, well hopped and with a fairly high alcohol content.

India Pale Ales were originally made extra strong so that they would stand up to the rigours of long sea journeys, with the constant movement and varying temperatures that were unavoidable in transporting beer, from the 1820s onwards, to the troops in India and other distant parts of the British Empire. The taste for this type of beer was brought back by returning servicemen, and IPAs have been a popular British bottled beer ever since. To achieve the fine, delicate hop bouquet, only the finest quality Golding hops are used. The dry, grainy flavour comes from using the very best of pale malts, with adjuncts such as flaked rice and wheat syrup. Higher than average mash tun temperatures bring about a high dextrin beer. As dextrins are slow to ferment, the beer continues to improve and gain carbonation during its storage time. Old-style bottled beers were all naturally conditioned. This simply means that the beer was bottled with a continuing slight fermentation, and this made the beer slightly gassy. The finest quality beers were all conditioned this way, just as the finest sparkling wines are bottle-conditioned. Modern brewery bottled beers are almost all sterile, lifeless brews, artificially carbonated just as though they were fizzy soft drinks. Indeed, a few of them are approaching that low alcohol level, just above two per cent.

It may be difficult for amateur brewers to obtain the top quality ingredients, but using the best available to you will ensure that you produce beers that will match anything but the most expensive of commercial brews.

If this is your first venture into home brewing, then this simple way of making beer is well worth a try.

Bitter Beer

(3 gallons/13.5 litres)

1 can hopped malt extract syrup for 24 pts/13.5ltrs of bitter or pale ale.
½lb/250g sugar
Beer yeast, if not provided
Water to make up to 3gall/13.5ltr

There are many reputable brands of beer kit on the market, mostly in 24 or 40 pint sizes. Each brand of beer kit carries its own instructions, but a reasonable bitter can be made quite easily this way. First of all, sterilise a new five-gallon bucket or fermenting bin with Campden tablets or sodium metabisulphite solution, and then add cold water a gallon at a time, marking each level on the outside of the bin. Empty the bin, and make each gallon-level marking permanent with a laundry marking pen or similar.

Warm the can of extract in a bowl of hot water; this makes the malt extract easier to get out of the can and to dissolve in the water. Pour 4 pints/2.25 litres of water into a large pan, and heat to near boiling point. **(1)** Add the malt extract, rinsing out the can with hot water to get all the extract into the pan. Stir well, and bring back up to near boiling point. Stir in the sugar, making sure it is all dissolved, then simmer gently for ten minutes. **(2)** Empty the contents of the pan into the sterilised bin, and add cold water to bring the level up to the 3 gallon/13.5 litre mark. **(3)** When the wort feels just cool about 20°C (70°F), **(4)** sprinkle the dried yeast on the surface. Cover the bin with a lid or sheet of polythene to exclude airborne infections, flies etc., and leave for twenty-four hours for the fermentation to start. The wort will quickly build up a layer of froth, usually with a brown 'tidemark' round the edge of the bin. **(5)** The froth and the brown ring should be skimmed off, to prevent the beer from having an excessively bitter flavour.

1

2

3

4

5

Keep the bin in a warm room. Stir the wort thoroughly each day for four or five days, by which time the beer should have ceased throwing up a froth and the bubbling slowed down to almost nothing. **(6)** It helps at this stage to transfer the young beer to 1 gallon/4.5 litre jars to protect it from wild yeasts that would spoil it.

The beer should fall clear within another three or four days; if it does not, add some proprietary beer finings in accordance with the maker's instructions. Syphon the clear beer off into another container; **(7)** if you have a hydrometer, the beer should have a specific gravity of 1050 or less. Add 12 teaspoons/60 grams of sugar, dissolved in a little hot water, and stir well to ensure even dispersion. The beer can then be bottled, in ordinary glass bottles, or the P.E.T. plastic bottles used for beer and other fizzy drinks. Make sure they are sterilised before use, and fill to within 1-1½ inches/25-30 mm of the top. **(8)** Screw the lids down firmly, or seal with metal or plastic crown caps as appropriate.

Store the finished beer in the warm for three days, for the yeast to give it that little extra sparkle, then store for three weeks in a cool place. Your first beer should by then be in perfect condition.

❑ *Using soft brown sugar instead of white will make quite a difference to the beer; try it in the next batch from this recipe.*

6

7

8

Larger batches of beer are just as easy to make, and give greater scope for experiment. Unfortunately, larger batches seem to last no longer than smaller ones! Try this basic five-gallon brew recipe:-

Bitter Beer

(5 gallons/22.5 litres)

6 b/2.7k pale dried malt extract

1lb/450g sugar

4oz/125g crystal malt

4oz/125g Goldings hops

(1) Boil the malt extract and 3 ounces/30 grams of the hops in 1 gallon/4.5 litres of water for 15 minutes. **(2)** Strain into the fermenting bin, **(3)** sparge (pour hot water over) the hops to wash out any remaining malt sugars, and stir in the granulated sugar. **(4)** Tie the remainder of the hops in a piece of muslin, and add them to the bin. **(5)** Make up to 5 gallons/22.5 litres with cold water and **(6)** sprinkle the yeast over the surface. Cover and leave to ferment. **(7)** Skim daily to remove the excess hop bitters and yeast foam, and stir well each time. After three days, put under airlock to protect the beer from wild yeasts. When the fermentation has died down, remove the bag of hops. Add finings if the beer is not clearing naturally, and **(8)** rack it the following day. Stir in 4 ounces/125 grams of sugar dissolved in a little hot water, and either bottle in sterile bottles or in a keg as you prefer. Keep in a warm place for three or four days to condition (develop a sparkle), then store in the cool for two or three weeks to mature.

1

2

3

4

7

5

6

8

Most commercial beer is produced from malted barley grains, not the extract of malted grain used by the great majority of amateur brewers. The grain beers are often the best beers – many competition successes tend to support this – so here is a pale malt barley recipe to try:

Bitter Beer

(5 gallons)

5lb/2.25kg crushed pale malt (buy ready milled)
4oz/125g crushed crystal malt (chop in a blender)
4oz/125g brewing flour
2oz/60g Fuggles hops
1oz/30g Goldings hops
1tsp/5g Irish moss (copper finings)
8oz/250g white sugar
8oz/250g Demerara sugar
Top-fermenting beer yeast

1

2

3

4

A good homebrew shop should supply crushed malt. If not, reduce it to small particles with a coffee mill or coarse mincer. Do not reduce the malt to flour as this may lead to poor results. **(1)** Put 5 pints/2.5 litres of water in a large pan with the crushed pale malt, **(2)** the crystal malt, **(3)** and the brewing flour. Add a little more water if necessary; it should be of a **(4)** runny porridge consistency. Bring to the boil and simmer gently for one hour. Keep as near to 66°C (150°F) as possible, stirring frequently to prevent it sticking. **(5)** Tip the mash into a large sieve lined with muslin, over the fermenting bin. When the wort has strained through, **(6)** sparge (sprinkle) the malt residue with a kettleful of hot water to wash out any residual malt sugars. Tip the wort back into the pan, **(7)** add the hops and Irish moss, which helps clarify the beer, and boil for half an hour. **(8)** Pour it back into the bin through a sieve, **(9)** add the sugars and **(10)** stir well to dissolve them. Make up to 5 gallons/22.5 litres with cold water. When cool, 21°C (70°F), **(11)** add the yeast **(12)** and cover. **(13)** Skim off the foam daily for up to four days, then rack (syphon off the

5

sediment) and keep under airlock. After seven days add beer finings, **(14)** and rack the next day into a keg. Stir in 4 ounces/125 grams of sugar as a syrup, and bottle the beer, or cap the keg. This should be an excellent bitter in three weeks or so.

6

7

8

9

10

11

12

13

14

Pale Ale

(5 gallons/22.5 litres)

4lb/1.8kg dried pale malt extract
2lb/900g glucose
2oz/60g cracked crystal malt
3oz/90g Goldings hops (or 2oz/60g Hallertauer)

Boil all ingredients for 30 minutes in 1 gallon/4.5 litres of water, and strain onto 1 pound/450 grams of white sugar. Sparge the hops and crystal malt remains by sprinkling a kettleful of hot water over them to wash out the last of the malt sugars. Stir well, then add cold water to the 5 gallon/22.5 litre mark. When cool add the yeast and cover the bin with its lid or polythene tied in place. Skim the foam off daily after the first day, and after five days transfer the wort to a container or demijohns where it can be protected by airlocks.

Below: neatly packed bales of hops. Facing page: oasts silhouetted against a glowing sunset.

Pale Ale

(5 gallons/22.5 litres)

5lb/2.25kg light dried malt extract
2¼lb/1kg sugar
2oz/60g East Kent Goldings hops
Beer yeast

Boil the malt and hops in 1 gallon/2.5 litres of water for 20 minutes, in two batches if you haven't a big enough pan. Strain into a 5 gallon/22.5 litre fermenter and sparge the hops with a kettleful of hot water, then discard them. Stir in the sugar until dissolved. Add 3 gallons/13.5 litres of cold water and, when the wort is cool, add the yeast and cover closely. Skim daily for three days, rousing well (i.e.stirring vigorously) each time. After three days put under airlock in a keg or demijohns, and leave to ferment out. Rack the beer off the sediment and stir in 4 ounces/125 grams of sugar dissolved in a little hot water. Bottle and store for a few days in the warm, then move into a cold room for two or three weeks at least before drinking.

Pale Ale

(5 gallons/22.5 litres)

6lb/2.7kg crushed pale malt
2¼lb/1kg soft brown sugar
4oz/125g crushed crystal malt
3oz/90g East Kent Goldings hops
Top-fermenting beer yeast

Boil ingredients in 1 gallon/2.5 litres of water, and simmer for twenty minutes. Strain into the fermenting bin, sparge the hops and spent grains, and add water to 5 gallons/22.5 litres. Pitch the yeast when cool, and then skim the foam daily for three days. Rack the beer into a 5 gallon/22.5 litre container and fit an airlock. At the end of seven days from the start, add finings and rack the next day. Use 4 ounces/125 grams sugar dissolved in hot water to prime the brew after fining and racking, then bottle. Ready to drink in three weeks.

❑ *This recipe also copies the brewers, in using malted barley, not extract.*

History of Lager

Although so-called lager beers have rapidly become popular in the UK in the last few years, lagers are of ancient origin, having been brewed in Munich since at least 1420 AD. From there it spread across Europe and much of the world, and now probably more lager is produced than all other beer types together. British top-fermenting beer yeast is Saccharomyces cerevisiae, but most commercial lagers are brewed with a special strain of yeast, Saccharomyces carlsbergensis. Some of this specialised bottom-fermenting yeast strain was taken in 1845 from Munich to the Carlsberg Brewery in Denmark, where in 1883 Hansen succeeded in isolating a single yeast cell, from which the pure Carlsbergensis strain was cultivated. Instead of patenting his yeast production system, Hansen made it available to all brewers free of cost, an act of true altruism, for he renounced a fortune and benefited brewers all over the world.

True lagers are made by a system known as double-decoction, where instead of continuously heating the whole mash, a portion is extracted, raised to a high temperature, and returned to the bulk of the brew. The fermentation is carried on at a lower temperature than with top-fermenting yeasts, and because of this the brew is open to infection for a longer period. This is the reason for lagers being made from a particularly pure strain of yeast, so infection is less likely to occur. The comparatively long storage and maturation time that is given to lagers gave rise to their name, which means 'store'.

The hops used in lager making are the Continental varieties, such as Hallertau, Saaz, or Styrian Goldings, which are grown as female plants only and thus do not give rise to seeds. This means a cleaner, fresh nose and flavour, and it has been suggested that absence of seeds means that the beers are not as sleep-inducing as beers made from seed-bearing hop cones, as used in the UK.

The malts also differ, in that they are paler malts than is usual in Britain, and the fermenting temperature is lower, in the range 6°C (43°F) to 12°C (54°F). The liquor (water) should be fairly soft. Make your best lagers within these parameters, and you will make lagers that make your local pub's beers seem like children's pop by comparison. The main points are to ferment coolly, using a lager yeast and very pale (lager) malt, Hallertau or Saaz hops, which are now easily available, and be prepared to let your bottled lager rest and mature in a cool storeplace for at least two months. Of course, the beer can be drunk earlier than this, but it is strongly recommended that at least part of the brew is put away in an convenient store, to mature and grow into a superb lager for your enjoyment.

The main type of lager sold in the UK is Pilsen, originating in Czechoslovakia, but there are many other types. At the other end of the range are the Munich beers, which tend to be heavy, dark brews, quite different from the usual lagers sold in Great Britain.

Lager

(4 gallons/18 litres)

4lb/1.8kg can of hopped lager malt

extract (Vina, Paines, Munton, EDME etc.)

1lb/450g pale golden sugar

1oz/30g Goldings lager yeast – bottom fermenting

Dissolve the malt and sugar in 1 gallon/ 4.5 litres of boiling water, and simmer for twenty minutes. Transfer to your fermenting bin, make up to 4 gallons/18 litres with cold water, and add the yeast when the wort is cool, 24°C (75°F). Cover and allow to ferment; after two days, add the hops in a muslin bag so that they can easily be removed later. After the bubbles have stopped rising (SG 1005 or less), remove the hops and add beer finings according to maker's instructions. One day later the lager can be racked (syphoned off the yeast sediment), primed by stirring in 4 ounces/125 grams of sugar dissolved in a little hot water, and bottled. Leave for a week in the warm to condition (develop a sparkle), then store for another two weeks in the cooler part of the house or in the garage.

❏ *A nice and easy lager to start with, made from a kit.*

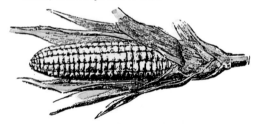

Lager

(5 gallons/22.5 litres)

4lb/1.8kg pale dried malt extract

2oz/75g Saaz or Hallertauer hops

1lb/450g granulated white sugar

Lager (bottom fermenting) yeast

Good seedless Continental hops are not always available from local suppliers. If you have difficulty, substitute 4 ounces/ 125 grams of the best Goldings you can buy.

Dissolve the malt extract in 1 gallon/ 4.5 litres of hot water, bring to the boil and add the hops. If your pan is not big enough, divide both the hops and malt into two batches. Let them boil for twenty minutes.

Pour the liquor through a strainer into a 5 gallon/22.5 litre bucket or bin, and sprinkle the hops in the strainer with a kettle of hot water to ensure the trapped malt solution is rinsed out. Add the sugar, and stir until dissolved. Add 3¢ gallons/ 16 litres of cold water, and when the temperature is down to 24°C (75°F) or less – just nicely cool – add the yeast and cover the bin to exclude bacteria etc.

After three days, syphon off into a 5 gallon/22.5 litre fermenter or five demijohns, and protect with airlock(s) until the beer has cleared. Rack off into a keg, and make up to 5 gallons/22.5 litres with water. Stir in 4 ounces/125 grams of sugar dissolved in hot water, then screw down the keg cap. This brew should be clear after two or three weeks, but if in doubt add proprietary finings to the barrel.

Lager

(5 gallons/22.5 litres)

5lbs/2.25kg crushed lager malt

⅓lb/175g flaked maize

2½oz/75g Hallertauer or 4oz/125g East Kent Goldings hops

1tsp/5g Irish moss

Lager yeast

Flaked maize can usually be bought from health food stores if your homebrew supplier doesn't stock it. If necessary, you can substitute ⅓ pound/175 grams of flaked rice or 1 pound/450 grams of cornflakes, though this will slightly alter the character of the lager.

Put the malt and flakes in a large pan, and add hot water slowly until the mash has a sloppy, porridge-like consistency. Heat up to 55°C (130°F), stirring continuously, then leave off the heat for half an hour. Reheat to the same temperature, stirring as before, and allow to stand for another half hour. Finally, reheat to 65°C (150°F), remove from the heat and allow to stand and cool.

Spread a muslin or nylon cloth on a large strainer over the fermenting vessel, and tip the contents of the pan onto this. Sparge (rinse with a sprinkle of hot water) until you have about 2 gallons/9 litres in total.

Remove the strainer and boil the sweet wort up, in two batches if necessary, with the hops and Irish moss for an hour. Strain again into the fermenter, make up to 5 gallons/22.5 litres with cold water, and add the yeast when the brew has cooled. Cover, and ferment in a warm place until the fermentaion has ended and the bubbles have almost stopped rising. Then rack off (syphon) into airlocked container(s) for a week. The lager can then be primed by stirring in 4 ounces/125 grams of sugar dissolved in a little hot water, and either run into a keg as a draught lager, or bottled in suitable bottles. Allow this lager three days in the warm to condition, and at least three weeks to mature in cool storage.

Lager

(1 gallon/4.5 litres)

2lb/900g dark dried malt extract

1oz/30g crushed crystal malt

1oz/30g Fuggles or ½oz/15g Hallertauer hops

Lager yeast

(1) Boil the malt extract, **(2)** crystal malt and **(3)** hops in ⅓ gallon/3.3 litres of water for about half an hour, **(4)** then strain into a bucket. Cover and leave to cool, **(5)** then pour through a funnel into a demijohn and **(6)** add the lager yeast. **(7)** Fit the airlock and leave to ferment for five days. Top up with cold water, and leave again for another five days. Syphon the clear beer off the sediment and bottle, adding ½ teaspoon/3 grams of sugar to each bottle before filling. Store in the warmth for three days, then in the cool for a fortnight.

❑ *The dark, Munich-style lagers are not well known in the UK, so this is a recipe to try on a small scale.*

1

2

3

4

5

6

7

Mild and Brown Ales, Cider and Perry

Mild beer once accounted for over half the total output of British beers, but from the 1950s onwards it suffered a drastic decline. Bitters and pale ales became fashionable, and more recent years have seen the lager market making further inroads into sales to the mild-drinking public. Many breweries have severely curtailed their mild production in favour of the lighter coloured beers, despite the fact that mild beer is a more economical product to make. Commercial mild is also a fairly low alcohol beer, a good selling point in these safety-conscious days, and it might be thought that these two reasons alone would revive its flagging popularity.

Mild beer is made partly from the same pale malt that bitter is brewed with, plus a proportion of a darker, more heavily-kilned malt to give it some colour, notably amber malt. It does vary greatly in depth of hue, tending to a deepish brown in the southern counties, especially around London, and becoming paler in the Midlands and north. It has a lower hopping rate than the other beers, and is altogether a softer and easier beer to drink. It also has the advantage that it is quick maturing; a basic beer for quenching thirsts, it is not noted for its strong nose or complex flavour. It would be pointless maturing it for months, for it would not improve greatly. A popular brew, it is meant to be drunk in pints for satisfaction rather than contemplation.

Brown ale is mostly mild beer that has been bottled. It is usually filtered and pasteurised to prevent refermentation, sweetened, and carbonated when bottled. An excellent northern example is Newcastle Brown, which is paler coloured than even some of the southern draught bitters. Most brown ales are soft, sweet, low-hopped beers, and an ideal introduction to drinking if you find the bitter flavour of the stronger and paler beers not to your taste.

For a first attempt at cider making, it is recommended that you buy a can of apple cider concentrate, which will be a balanced blend adjusted for acid and tannins. The instructions are simple to follow, and the resulting beverage is certainly better than the majority of the bland, semi-sweet commercial bottled ciders advertised nationally. Cider apples are generally only available in the counties from Hereford to the south coast, but there is no reason why cider should not be made successfully throughout Britain from blends of crab, dessert and cooking apples. High acid apples, such as Bramleys, are 'sharp', and crabs are known as 'bitters' for their high tannin content. Between them they should provide the necessary flavour, tannins and sharpness found in specialised cider apples – indeed, much commercial cider has its base in what are commonly regarded as eating apples. If you would like to grow your own cider apple trees, look for the specialised strains, which have fascinating names like Foxwhelp,

Dabinette, and Brown Snout. On a historical note, the fermented juice of simple apples, without added water or sugar, gives the ancient and honourable drink of 'cyder', and the diluted, adjusted and carbonated brews that have succeeded the original English beverage have been titled 'cider', a vastly different drink.

Perry is strictly the fermented juice of pears, and there are very few true perries now on sale. Comparatively low in alcohol compared with wine, perry can be sweet or dry, still or sparkling. Pears are high in tannin, but low in acid and nutrients, and the addition of a teaspoon each of tartaric acid and ammonium phosphate (or a branded nutrient) per 1 gallon/4.5 litres is advisable. If you have a pear tree that produces hard, almost inedible fruit that doesn't soften and ripen with storage, it may well be worth coarsely mincing or crushing the fruit and trying your hand at making a gallon or two of perry. You could well be delighted with the result.

Mild Beer

(1 gallon/4.5 litres)

1lb/450g dark malt extract

3oz/90g cracked crystal malt

1tsp/5ml caramel

½tsp/3g salt

1oz/30g Fuggles hops

2tsp/10g low-calorie granulated sweetener (Canderel or similar)

Top-fermenting beer yeast

Place all ingredients except the sweetener and yeast into a pan with ½ gallon/2.25 litres of water and bring to the boil. Simmer gently for fifteen minutes, then strain into a bucket. Sprinkle 2 pints/1 litre of hot water over the strainer contents to recover the last of the malt sugar, collecting the drainings in the bucket. Cover and leave to cool. Discard the exhausted contents of the strainer.

When the wort has cooled, pour it through a funnel into a 1 gallon/4.5 litre jar, and add the yeast and sweetener. Fit the bung and airlock, and leave to ferment for three or four days. Then top up to the full gallon/4.5 litres, and allow the fermentation to continue. When bubbles are no longer rising in quantity, syphon the beer off the sediment, and add 4 teaspoons/20 grams of sugar dissolved in a little hot water; top up to the gallon/4.5 litres if necessary with cold water and bottle. Store in the warm for three days to gain some sparkle, then put the bottles away for a fortnight before drinking their contents.

❏ *Mild beers vary considerably around the country, and are often confused with brown ales as they can have similar characteristics. Here is an easy recipe for just 1 gallon/4.5 litres of mild beer.*

Mild Beer

(5 gallons/ 22.5 litres)

3½lb/1.6kg dark malt extract

½lb/250g cracked crystal malt

3oz/90g Fuggles hops

1tblsp/30ml caramel

1tsp/5g salt

Top fermenting beer yeast

Place all ingredients except the yeast in a large pan, and bring to the boil with 1 gallon/4.5 litres of water; simmer for half an hour, then strain into the fermenting bin. Sparge (sprinkle with hot water) the contents of the strainer, to obtain the last of the malt sugars. Make up to 5 gallons/ 22.5 litres with cold water, and when cool add the yeast. Cover and leave in a warm place to ferment for four days. Then syphon off the sediment into another container or demijohns that can be fitted with airlocks. Leave to finish fermenting, then stir in 4 teaspoons/20 grams of non-sugar granulated sweetener, or five saccharine tablets. Also stir in 4 ounces/25 grams of sugar dissolved in a little hot water to give the beer a sparkle. This is a draught ale for dispensing from a keg, but if you prefer it can be bottled. Bottle in pressure-resistant bottles, keep in the warm for three days to condition, and mature for two to three weeks in a cool store.

Brown Ale

(1 gallon/4.5 litres)

12oz/375g dark malt syrup, or 10oz/310g dark dried malt

4oz/125g brown sugar

2oz/60g cracked crystal malt

1oz/30g Fuggles hops

Top-fermenting beer yeast

Put all except the yeast in a pan with ½ gallon/2.25 litres of water, bring to the boil, then simmer for half an hour. Strain into the fermenting bucket, and sparge the hops and grain husks with 2 pints/1 litre of hot water. Add 1½ pints/800 ml of cold water, cover, and leave to cool. Next, transfer the wort to a demijohn and add the yeast. Fit the bung and airlock, and leave in the warm to ferment for a week. Rack off the sediment, rinse the jar and return the beer to it. Add a couple of crushed saccharine tablets, and 4 teaspoons/125 grams of sugar dissolved in a little hot water. Top up to a full gallon/4.5 litres with cold water, and bottle. Keep the beer warm for three days to condition, then store in the cool for a fortnight before sampling.

Once bottled, the beer is sealed with crown caps.

Brown Ale

(5 gallons/22.5 litres)

7lb/3.15kg crushed pale malt grains

12oz/375g cracked crystal malt

1lb/450g dark brown sugar

4oz/125g Goldings hops

1tsp/5g of Irish moss finings

10tsp/50g granulated non-fermenting sweetener (Canderel or similar)

Top-fermenting beer yeast

Stir the malts into 1 gallon/4.5 litres of water at 65°C (150°F), and keep at this temperature for one-and-a-half hours, stirring frequently. Strain through muslin into the fermenting bin, and sparge with a kettleful of hot water to release the trapped maltose. Discard the contents of the strainer.

Boil the liquor with the sugar, 3 ounces/100 grams of the hops, and the Irish moss for half an hour. Make the liquor up to 5 gallons/22.5 litres with cold water. When cooled to 24°C (75°F) add the yeast, the other 1 ounce/30 grams of hops, and the sweetener. Cover, and leave in a warm place to ferment for three days. Strain the hops out, then rack into container(s) protected by airlock(s). Store for a further week, add finings if still cloudy, and a couple of days later syphon off any thick sediment and stir in 4 ounces/125 grams of sugar as a solution in hot water. Bottle at once, keep warm for three days, then store for at least three weeks in the cool to mature and improve.

❑ *This is a 'Newcastle Brown' type of beer, though not an exact replica. Drier and less soft-textured than the brown ales from the southern parts of England, it is lighter in colour and higher in alcohol, though still full-bodied.*

Brown Ale

(5 gallons/22.5 litres)

3lb/1.6kg dark malt

3oz/90g Fuggles hops

1½lb/700g dark brown sugar

10oz/310g cracked crystal malt

12oz/375g lactose

Top-fermenting beer yeast

(1) Simmer all ingredients (except yeast) in 1 gallon/4.5 litres of water for half an hour, **(2)** then strain into the fermenting bin. **(3)** Spray the contents of the strainer with a kettle of hot water to wash out the residue of malt sugars; these will also drain into the fermenter. Discard the strainer contents. Add 3 gallons/13.5 litres of cold water, **(4)** sprinkle yeast over the surface when the brew is cool, **(5)** and cover the bin to protect from wild yeasts etc. Ferment in a warm place for four days, **(6)** then transfer to a container or demijohns where airlocks can protect the brew from infections or spoilage yeasts. Three days later add finings, and on the eighth day syphon the young beer off the sediment. Stir in 4 ounces/125 grams of sugar dissolved in a little warm water, **(7)** bottle the beer and store it in the warm for a few days to develop a sparkle. Then keep the bottles for a further two weeks in the cool to mature before drinking.

❑ *If you cannot buy dark malt, either buy pale malt extract and add a tablespoon of caramel to the mash, or use a mild ale kit and omit the hops.*

1

2

3

4

5

6

7

Perry
(1 gallon/4.5 litres)

Perry is the pear-based equivalent of cider and, like cider, is a natural wine of the country, from fruit that grows prolifically and well in Britain and has been made for centuries. Some varieties of pear date back at least to Roman times, but one of the best, Laxton's Superb, may not now be grown because of its susceptibility to fire blight.

Perry recipes are few and far between, as are the pears grown for perry making; these are mainly found in the Midland region and counties to its south. The common dessert pear varieties are low in acid, and blending with a few sharp apples is recommended. Pears have skins high in tannin, so it is suggested that the pears are not pressed until at least twenty-four hours after they have been crushed. Alternatively, half the pear skins can be peeled off and discarded. A typical recipe for the home winemaker without supplies of the special perry pears would be:

10lb/4.5kg pears
10lb/4.5kg mixed apples
1lb/450g sugar
2tsp/10g pectic enzyme

Wash the fruit in a sulphite solution (2 Campden tablets per 1 gallon/4.5 litres), then freeze and thaw, or simply crush the fruit, and press the juice out. Dissolve the sugar in ½ pint/280 ml of hot water, and stir it into the juice. Pour into a demijohn, add a good wine yeast and the pectic enzyme, and fit the rubber bung and airlock. Syphon the must off the sediment after a fortnight, top up to the gallon/4.5 litre mark with tap water, and leave for the fermentation to be completed. Rack again, when the perry falls clear, on to a crushed Campden tablet, and bottle. Store for at least a month before sampling, longer if you can resist it.

Cider

Cider (1 gallon/4.5 litres)

This is cider made the farmhouse way. If you have lots of suitable apples, simply multiply the figures by the number of gallons/litres to be made.

Take approximately 20 pounds/9 kilos of apples to produce 1 gallon/4.5 litres of cider. If you have only bland dessert apples, the addition of a couple of pounds of pears, complete with skins, or ¼ teaspoon/1 gram of grape tannin per gallon/4.5 litres, is recommended. Let the apples mature and soften for a couple of weeks before crushing them; they will have a fine fruity smell, wrinkled skins, and after crushing will press easily. Add a crushed Campden tablet to each gallon/ 4.5 litres of juice. If the specific gravity is less than 1040, stir in a solution of granulated white sugar to increase the gravity to 1040-1060. Put the juice, 1 teaspoon/5 grams of pectic enzyme per gallon/4.5 litres, and a general purpose wine yeast into a 1 gallon/4.5 litre jar, or multiples thereof, and fit an airlock and rubber bung. Leave to ferment to dry, rack (syphon off the sediment), add a crushed Campden tablet, and bottle. If a sweeter cider is required, sweeten to taste with a non-fermenting granulated sweetener such as granulated Canderel, Nutrasweet or similar,or a winemaker's proprietary non-fermenting sweetener, which is usually based on saccharine and glycerol. Saccharine alone tends to leave a bitter aftertaste.

Sparkling cider can easily be made by bottling the cider when the specific gravity reading is 1005 or less. However, any such drink must be bottled solely in bottles intended for sparkling drinks, such as beer, sparkling cider, or lemonade. P.E.T. plastic bottles are safe and easily obtained. 'One-use' non-returnable glass bottles are not suitable, and should be consigned to the dustbin for safety's sake.

cider

(1 gallon/4.5 litres)

Accumulate in the deep-freeze 17-18 pounds/8 kilos of **(1)** assorted apples – green windfalls, desserts, crabs, cookers – the more mixed the better, but rinse them in a Campden tablet solution first. Fast freezing is not required, rather slow freezing to cause large destructive ice crystals in the fruit is advantageous, as the ruptured cells in the fruit give a larger juice extract. When all the apples have had at least twenty-four hours freezing, place them in a large bucket to thaw. Don't just leave them around in bags to thaw, or part of the valuable juice will be lost.

(2) Press the thawed fruit, or **(3)** crush and squeeze with a twisted cloth to extract the juice. Dose this at once with a crushed **(4)** Campden tablet or 1 teaspoon/5 ml of sulphite solution to prevent oxidation, and a pectic enzyme in accordance with the manufacturer's instructions. If you have an hydrometer, dissolve 1 pound/450 grams of sugar in ½ pint/280 ml of boiling water and let it cool. Use this little by little to increase the specific gravity of the juice to between SG 1040 and SG 1060. If you don't have an hydrometer, add 4 ounces/125 grams of sugar dissolved in hot water; this should give your cider a minimum alcohol content of 4 per cent, which is slightly higher than the average pub beer.

(5) Add a general purpose wine yeast to ensure that fermentation takes place. Usually the wild yeast on the apples will take care of this, but cultivated yeasts are more reliable and give a better end product. **(6)** Ferment the juice in a demijohn with a bung and airlock fitted, and rack it off the sediment after two weeks. **(7)** The brew can then be topped up to the full gallon/4.5 litres again with cold water, **(8)** and left for the fermentation to come to an end. The cider will slowly clear from the surface downwards, when all is clear it should be syphoned off any sediment that may have formed. Add a crushed Campden tablet, and put the cider away to mature for a month or so.

1

2

3

4

5

6

7

8

Strong Ales and Stout, Porter and Mulls

Strong ales, heavy beers, old ales, barley wines: all are descriptions of strong beers, usually with an original gravity of 1060 or more, sometimes – but rarely – with an alcohol content of over ten per cent by volume. When produced by commercial breweries they are often made for a special occasion, such as a brewery bicentennial or a royal wedding. Strong ales are also available from some brewers as winter specials, generally known as 'Owd Tom', 'Old Ben' or some other distinguishing name that puts them apart from the usual draught beers. Because of their high alcohol content – a nip of 'Imperial Stout' is said to be as strong as two measures of whisky! – these beers are usually sold in small bottles, from 17 to 27.5cl, and with their smooth finish and warming effect are seductively easy to drink.

Stout appeared in the seventeenth century, originally in its old meaning of strong, being the first run off the mashed grain. 'Stout Butt Beer' was the finest beer then available. Much amber malt was used in those days, and the method of malting meant that much of the malt was over-carbonised, and slightly charred, giving the beer a harsh, dark finish that took time to dispel. The same depth of colour and flavour was later obtained by including 'Patent Black' malt in the brew; nowadays this has been replaced by the inclusion of roasted, unmalted barley, which gives a smoother finish and equal depth of colour. Apart from the variation in ingredients, stout is made in just the same way as any other top-fermented beer, but the malts used tend to give it a closer and longer-lasting head.

Porter is another ancient brew that certain manufacturers and brewers are now trying to revive. Said to have originated at the Bell Brewhouse in Shoreditch in 1722, porter became very popular, replacing the 'three threads' that was a common drink at the time. Because beer has a limited barrel life, it was then the custom to serve a blend, probably of pale ale, new brown ale and stale brown ale, to prevent too much wastage. Even this was an uneconomic practice, and a certain Ralph Harwood invented one beer to replace the three. Due to the labouring class customers of the area this became known as 'Porter', or 'Harwood's Entire', signifying the making of the whole brew into one beer, and not splitting it into differing grades as the mash was reused. Porter eventually faded away, ousted by the invention of Wheeler's Patent for malting, mentioned previously under 'Stout', and the growth in production of pale ales which, being more highly hopped than sweet brown ales, had paid an unfair amount of the 'hop tax'. As this was reduced, and then finally abolished, in the nineteenth century, so pale ales and bitters became cheaper by comparison with porter and other brown ales, and eventually superseded them.

Mulls are not a type of beer, but a way of preparing a beer for drinking. The process varies from place to place, and period to period, but the basic idea is to add sugar and spices to beer, which is heated. The mulled ale is then drunk piping hot, and can be unhesitatingly recommended as a method of inducing a bodily glow that will drive out a cold, or at worst make it bearable. Pickwickian style Christmas cards often show ale being mulled by a poker heated in a tavern's roaring fire. This is fine if you don't have to drive home, but nowadays it is better to heat the beer in a saucepan on your cooker at home. Packets of ready-mixed mull spices can be bought, or you can try the recipe that follows at the end of this chapter.

Porter

(5 gallons/22.5 litres)

4lb/1.8kg dark malt extract

8oz/250g cracked crystal malt

8oz/250g crushed black malt

4oz/125g Fuggles hops

2lb/900g granulated white sugar

Boil all ingredients in 1 gallon/4.5 litres of water for half an hour, then strain liquid into a 5 gallon/22.5 litre fermenting bin. Sparge (sprinkle) the hops and grain residue with a kettleful of hot water, then discard the solids. Make up to 5 gallons/22.5 litres with cold water, then add the beer yeast when cool. Cover, and stir daily for three days. Transfer the brew to a container protected by an airlock. Four days later, add finings, leave overnight, and rack the porter off the sediment. Stir in 4 ounces/125 grams of sugar dissolved in hot water, and store the porter in a keg to clear and mature. This draught beer can be drunk within a week or so if your barrel is fitted with a float for drawing the beer off from the surface.

Mulled Ale

Mulled ale is ideal for producing a warming glow on a cold winter's day, and is an ideal method of absorbing a little comforting liquid nourishment if suffering from a cold, or if you just feel you deserve it.

Traditionally, mulled ale was made by taking a red-hot poker from the public house fireplace and plunging it into a mug of beer containing sugar and spices, but this is not usually convenient in a modern household. Take a tankard of beer per head, preferably a nice mild beer or brown ale of your own making, and pour it into a pan. Heat it gently on the stove, with, for each mugful, a couple of teaspoonsful of brown sugar, a pinch each of powdered nutmeg and ginger, and a clove if you enjoy the flavour. Make the mixture hot, not boiling, and pour it into pewter mugs or preheated glass tankards. Sip this at bedtime while it is still piping hot, and a good night's rest is virtually guaranteed.

Christmas Special

| 2lbs/900g dark dried malt extract |
| 1lb/450g light dried malt extract |
| 1lb/450g cracked crystal malt |
| 4oz/125g Goldings hops |
| 2lb/900g brown sugar |
| 3lb/1.35kg white sugar |
| Good beer yeast |

(1) Boil the malts and hops in 1 gallon/ 4.5 litres of water for half an hour. **(2)** Strain over the fermenting bin, **(3)** sparge the solids with a couple of kettles of hot water, then discard them. Make the wort up to 4½ gallons/20 litres with cold water. When the wort has cooled, **(4)** sprinkle the yeast over the surface, and cover.

(5) This brew needs skimming if a heavy foam forms, **(6)** and any ring of brown scum should be wiped off the side of the bin with a sterile damp cloth. Give the beer a good stir daily, **(7)** and after four days syphon it into a container to **(8)** take an airlock. After a further week add isinglass beer finings as instructed by the manufacturer, and leave the beer undisturbed for another two days. Rack it off the yeast sediment, **(9)** and bottle with 4 ounces/125 grams of sugar stirred in to give the beer a sparkle. Keep the bottles in the warm for four days or so, then store in a cool cellar or garage for as long as you can resist it. At least three months maturation is recommended.

❏ *This beer really should be made six months before Christmas to give it time to mature. It is exceedingly strong, and is best bottled in halves or nips. It must be drunk with great caution, and should be avoided if you are likely to drive. It will keep in prime condition for at least ten years.*

1

2

3

4

5

6

7

8

9

Strong Ale

(1 gallon/4.5 litres)

| 1lb/450g dried dark malt extract |
| 4oz/125g crystal malt |
| 1lb/450g brown sugar |
| 1oz/30g black malt) |
| ¼tsp/1g Epsom salts |
| 1oz/30g Fuggles hops |
| Beer yeast |

Put all ingredients except yeast into a pan with 1 gallon/4.5 litres of water, and boil for half an hour. Strain off and leave to cool, with a cover to protect the wort. When cool, pour into a demijohn, and add a good beer yeast. Fit the bung and airlock and leave for fermentation to be completed, after about ten days. Rack off the sediment, and bottle with ½ teaspoon/2.5 grams of sugar per pint bottle. Keep the brew warm for three days, then put it to mature in the cool for three or four weeks to get the best from this beer,.

Malt Extract Dry Stout

(5 gallons/22.5 litres)

| 5lb/2.25kg dried malt extract |
| ½lb/250g cracked roasted barley |
| ½lb/250g coarsely ground black malt |
| 1lb/450g dark brown sugar |
| 4oz/125g Fuggles hops |
| 1tsp/5g of gypsum (optional) |
| Beer yeast |

Boil all except the yeast for half an hour in 1 gallon/4.5 litres of water, then strain the wort from the solids. Sparge (sprinkle with hot water) the hops, grain husks etc. to release any trapped sugars; the solids can then be discarded. Make up to 5 gallons/22.5 litres with cold water, when cooled add a good branded beer yeast, and cover the top of the bin with its lid, sheet polythene, or similar. Stir well daily, after skimming off any thick foam, and four days later syphon the brew into a container to which an airlock can be fitted. Leave for a further week, then rack the beer off the sediment and stir in 4 ounces/125 grams of sugar dissolved in a little hot water. The stout can then be put in a plastic barrel,or bottled in beer bottles or other pressure-resistant containers. Keep in the warm for four days to condition, i.e., for a sparkle to develop, then mature the stout for at least three weeks in a cool storeplace.

This stout lends itself well to conversion to a sweet stout, and this is done simply by dissolving 1 pound/450 grams of lactose sugar in some of the beer and stirring it in before bottling. Granulated non-sugar sweeteners such as Canderel can be used instead, and should be added at the rate of 1 teaspoon/5 grams per bottle. Sugar for conditioning is still rquired, as above.

Barley Malt Stout

(5 gallons/22.5 litres)

| 7lb/3.15kg crushed pale malt |
| 1lb/450g cracked roasted malt |
| ½lb/250g flaked maize |
| 3oz/90g Fuggles hops |
| Top-fermenting beer yeast |

Add all ingredients except the hops and yeast to 1½ gallons/6.75 litres boiling water and stir well. Adjust to 65°C (150°F), and hold there for a couple of hours. Strain out the solids, and sparge them with two kettles of boiling water, collecting the drainings in the fermenting bin with the rest of the wort. Return the wort to the pan, add the hops in a loose muslin bag, and boil for a further hour. Remove the hops, pour the wort into the fermenting bin, and top up to 5 gallons/ 22.5 litres with cold water. When cool add the yeast, and cover. Rouse (stir vigorously) each day, after skimming off any thick yeast foam, and syphon the stout off the sediment after three days, transferring it to an airlock-protected container. When the fermentation has ended, stir in 5 ounces/140 grams of sugar dissolved in a little hot water, and keg or bottle the beer in the usual way.

It is possible to culture the lees in a bottle of Guinness to provide the yeast for brewing stout at home. This can be done by allowing the stout to stand for twenty-four hours, then carefully pouring off about three-quarters of it and adding a little malt extract or sugar, dissolved in hot water and cooled, to the remaining quarter. Plug the bottle neck with a wad of unmedicated cotton wool, and keep it in the airing cupboard. Within forty-eight hours the bottle should be showing signs of yeast activity, in the form of tiny bubbles around the rim. The whole of the bottle's contents can then be used to start off your homebrew stout.

❑ *Only Guinness in returnable bottles is bottle conditioned and will contain yeast; Guinness in non-returnable bottles or cans is useless for this purpose, as it is sterile and yeast-free.*

Beer: Winning Prizes, and Prize-Winning Recipes

Home brewers have one great advantage over home winemakers when it comes to showing their bottles in competition: they are using the same ingredients as the professionals, whereas winemakers are, by and large, adapting the extracts from various fruits and flowers to match the juice extracted from the grape. It naturally follows that a home-brewed bitter, for example, may be identical with, or even better than, the commercial equivalent, whereas a home-made wine is unusual if it perfectly matches a professionally-produced grape wine.

The home brewer has many opportunities for putting his product to the test of being judged against other amateur beers; most horticultural and agricultural shows have competitive classes that are open to all comers. Anyone who has made a beer under hygienic conditions from a good recipe, with reasonably fresh ingredients, should stand every chance of winning an award at a show. There are a few points that are important:

1. Follow the recipe, or the manufacturer's instructions, implicitly, at least in your first few brews.

2. Ensure that all equipment, at every stage, is scrupulously clean. Use a branded cleanser/sterilant.

3. Don't try to hurry matters. Given time, your beer should clear brilliantly. Rack it off any sediment before you try to bottle it; there will always be sufficient yeast in suspension to cause a secondary fermentation in the bottle. The beer that is bottled while still cloudy will throw a deep, soft deposit in the bottom of the bottle; this will be obvious to the judge and you will lose points both for presentation and clarity.

4. Do ensure that you follow the show rules precisely. These are always supplied to every show exhibitor, and are designed expressly to prevent the inadvertent recognition of any exhibit by the judge, by standardising the appearance of all the bottles. You must always use the bottle label as supplied or instructed, the standard bottle and type of closure prescribed by the organisers, and fill the bottle to within the specified limits. If not stated, the surface of the beer is usually to be within 1 inch/25 mm, and certainly not less than half that, of the bottom of the closure. Apart from the label bearing the exhibitors' identifying numbers by which only the show secretary can know the entrants, all the bottles should be identical in appearance.

5. The bottle must be scrupulously clean inside and out; when you clean and sterilise the bottle, rinse it with fresh water, shake it free of excess, and fill it with the beer at once. This prevents watermarks being left inside the bottle as it dries.

IPA ~ India Pale Ale

(Mr P. Hardy, NGWBJ)

To make 5 gallons/22.5 litres

10lb/4.5kg pale malt grain, coarsely ground.
8oz/250g flaked barley
8oz/250g crystal malt, lightly crushed
1oz/30g roasted barley, lightly crushed
2½oz/75g East Kent Golding (EKG) hops
2½oz/75g Challenger hops
1oz further EKG or Styrian hops
Sachet of gelatine and ½oz/15g Irish moss
EDME beer yeast

Adjust the water to hard, and raise it to strike heat (i.e, the heat at which it is added to the malt) of 78°C (172°F),then mash for 2 hours at 65°C (150°F). Strain, and sparge until the runnings decrease to SG 1004. Bring to the boil, skimming off proteins, then add all except the last 1 ounce/30 grams of hops. Boil for an hour, adding the Irish Moss after 40 minutes, and the rest of the hops 5 minutes before the end to heighten the aroma. Leave it to stand for 20 minutes then turn out into the fermenter. Cool rapidly; if no suitable coil is available, stand the fermenter in cold water. Dilute to SG 1050 with cooled, boiled water. Add the EDME yeast when the temperature drops to 18°C (64°F).

Ferment down to SG 1012, then rack and add the gelatine finings. (Dissolve the gelatine by leaving it for a few minutes in a cup of hot water). Bottle after 5 days, adding sugar for conditioning at the rate of ½ teaspoon/3 grams per bottle. (If the beer is racked again, add 4 ounces/125 grams of sugar dissolved in a little hot water, stirring it well into the bulk beer.) leave the bottled beer in a warm place for 5 days, then remove it to a cool store for 6 weeks. This beer will continue to improve for up to 12 months.

The bottle should be free of any scratches, chips, gum smears from the label, or sticky fingerprints. Wiping the outside of the bottle the day before the show with a cloth dampened with methylated spirits, helps. This will remove any grubby marks, and the spirit will quickly evaporate. Polish the bottle with a clean dry cloth by all means, but please don't use any wax or silicone polish on it! A judge's life is hazardous enough already!

Most of the recipes already given in this book will produce beer of sufficient standard to put you among the winners in any local show, but to encourage you to make even finer beers, here are a few recipes that have won awards at the National or other major regional competitions in recent years.

Dry Stout

(Mr G. Sparrow, NGWBJ)

To make 4½ gallons/20 litres

7lb/3.15kg pale malt
1lb/450g roasted barley
8oz/250g flaked barley
8oz/250g torrified barley
5oz/150g black malt
1¼oz/35g Northern Brewer hops .
⅓oz/25g Bullion hops
½oz/15g Fuggles hops
Soft water treatment, plus ¼tsp/1g salt and ½tsp/3g calcium carbonate.
Beer (top fermenting) yeast

Add water treatment and boil water to start. Let it cool to 18°C (64°F), add the malt grist and other crushed grains, and mash for about one and a half to two hours, stirring frequently. Strain and sparge as described above, make up to 5 gallons/22.5 litres with cooled, boiled water, and cool quickly. Adjust with water, or sugar syrup if necessary, to a starting gravity of 1048. Ferment at 20°C (68°F), and rack when the gravity has dropped to SG 1012. Transfer to demijohns. Rack and bottle when fermentation has ended, with ½ teaspoon/3 grams of sugar per bottle, or 4 ounces/125 grams dissolved in hot water, stirred well into the recombined bulk beer, and add a little activated yeast. Store to condition at room temperature for three to five weeks, then store in the cool for drinking.

Brown Ale

To make 5 gallons/22.5 litres

1.5kg can dark malt extract
1½lb/700 g dark brown sugar
5oz/150g Fuggles hops.
12oz/375g crystal malt, coarsely cracked
2tsp/10ml caramel or gravy browning.
1lb/450g lactose sugar

Simmer all the ingredients in a large pan of water for 30 minutes. Strain into a fermenting bin, sparge strainings with a gallon of hot water, stir well. Make up to 5 gallons/22.5 litres with cooled, boiled water, and pitch the yeast when the wort has cooled to 21°C (70°F). It helps to activate the yeast in a little lukewarm water half an hour beforehand.

Ferment down to SG 1006, rack off the sediment, and stir in the lactose sugar and 5 fluid ounces/150 ml of sugar syrup. Bottle and keep in a warm place for 4 days, then store in the cold for at least 3 weeks.

❑ *Another malt extract beer, simple to make but of prize-winning quality.*

Owd Clog

(Mr R. Dutson, NGWBJ)

To make 4 gallons/18 litres.

2lb/900g light dried malt extract
1lb/450g dark dried malt extract
8oz/250g crystal malt grains
2oz/60g black malt grains
2lb/900g glucose chips or brewing sugar
2oz/60g Goldings hops
8oz/250g Cordon Brew Body
1 Nuhead
Beer yeast

This is a beer that has won many prizes in local shows, yet does not require extended mashing as it uses mainly malt extract. The Brew Body and Nuhead are to give the beer the characteristic body and creamy head that can only otherwise be obtained by mashing malted barley.

Take the largest pan you have, and place in it the crushed crystal malt and black malt grains, and 2 ounces/60 grams of the hops. Top up to 1 inch/25 mm below the rim with water, and bring to the boil. Continue to boil for 40 minutes, then add the rest of the hops and boil for a further 5 minutes.

Place the sugar and malt extracts and the Brew Body in the fermenting bin, strain the liquor from the pan over them, and sparge the straining residue with a kettle of hot water. Stir thoroughly until the malt and sugar are dissolved. Make up to 5 gallons/22.5 litres with cold water, and pitch the yeast when cooled to 21°C (70°F). Skim off the heavy yeast-laden foam that forms in the next couple of days, then leave the beer to ferment down to SG 1005, rack, and leave under airlock for a further two days. Then stir in 4 ounces/125 grams of sugar dissolved in a little hot water, and bottle. When bottled, keep the beer in a warm room for three or four days, then store in the cool for a further two or three weeks before drinking.

Manufacturers and wholesalers

There are many producers of wine and beer kits, but the major part of the market is held by a comparatively small number of brands and suppliers. Many small local groups of retailers sell their own brand of kit, especially beer kits, but again most of these are produced for them by the major manufacturers and labelled under the retailers' own brand or name.

The following manufacturers have all been in the trade for many years, and have built up reputations for good value and fair dealing. You may buy their products with confidence.

Your local homebrew retailer is bound to have a selection of producers' brands on offer, but it is unlikely (though not impossible) that he or she will carry everybody's range.

If you do not have a homebrew shop nearby, there are several retailers that sell by mail order, and who would gladly send you their catalogue. They all advertise in *Homebrew Today*, the free quarterly homebrew newspaper that retailers can obtain from their wholesaler. If you do not have a local shop, write to Homebrew Today Subscriptions, 4 Lytles Close, Formby, Liverpool L37 4BT for a sample copy and subscription details.

Cecil Vacuum Systems: Juice extractors.

CWE (Continental Wine Experts): Primarily producers of grape concentrate kits and grape and fruit extract kits for winemaking.

DDD Ltd: Makers of 'Chempro', a recommended cleaning and sterilising material for homebrewers.

EDME: Maltsters, producers of fine beer kits and malt extracts.

Hambleton Bard Ltd: Wholesale beer kits, malts, and pressure barrels and accessories. 'Danvino' brand wine kits.

Itona Product Ltd: A branch of Potters of Wigan, the herbalists. Makers of 'Kwoffit' beer and lager kits.

Johnson Homewine Supplies: Distributors of 'Vinamat' wine kits, filters, etc., and general suppliers of all things for homebrewing.

Munton & Fison plc: Maltsters, producing excellent beer kits and malts, under 'Munton's' brand.

Paine's Malts Ltd: Suppliers of malts and beer kits, best known under their brand name 'John Bull'.

Ritchie Products Ltd: Wholesale suppliers of most brands, plus a large and innovative range of own-brand goods.

Wander Foods Ltd: A subsidiary of 'Ovaltine', producing and wholesaling the famous 'Geordie' beer kits.

Vina (Home Winemaking Supplies) Ltd: One of the biggest wholesale firms in the trade, selling many other brands as well as their own house brands of 'Vina' products, 'Brewmaker', and Cumbria Home Brews'.

Youngs Home Brew: A Midland wholesale firm, selling all equipment and accessories, and a variety of brands of wine and beer kits, plus their own special wine kits under the 'Favourite' brand-name.